The High

Cookbook

Quick Simple Recipes to Prepare at Home

BY: SOPHIA FREEMAN

COPYRIGHTED

Liability

This publication is meant as an informational tool. The individual purchaser accepts all liability if damages occur because of following the directions or guidelines set out in this publication. The Author bears no responsibility for reparations caused by the misuse or misinterpretation of the content.

Copyright

The content of this publication is solely for entertainment purposes and is meant to be purchased by one individual. Permission is not given to any individual who copies, sells or distributes parts or the whole of this publication unless it is explicitly given by the Author in writing.

Table of Contents

Introduction

You're often told to eat more fiber.

You know it's important for your health. But do you know exactly why?

Dietary fiber, a component in plant-derived foods like vegetables, fruits, legumes and whole grains, is popular for its benefits for the digestive health.

Aside from promoting proper digestion and preventing digestive ailments such as constipation, fiber is also said to help reduce the risk of heart disease, diabetes and even some forms of cancer.

It is also known to help achieve or maintain a healthy weight.

Otherwise known as bulk or roughage, fiber comes in two types:

- Soluble fiber – This is the type of fiber that dissolves in water. It has been found to lower blood sugar and cholesterol levels. It can be found in peas, apples, carrots, barley, beans, oats, and citrus fruits, among others.
- Insoluble fiber – This type of fiber promotes proper bowel movement. Some of the best sources of this type of fiber include nuts, potatoes, cauliflower, wheat bran, whole wheat flour, beans and nuts.

According to the Institute of Medicine, adults are recommended to take in 25 to 30 grams of fiber each day.

In this cookbook, you'll get 50 high-fiber recipes that are not only flavorful and appetizing but are also quick and easy to make.

This way, even if you do not have the luxury of time to cook elaborate meals, you can still help maintain digestive health through simple high-fiber dishes.

Cheesy Apple Breakfast Sandwich

Here's a different take on your usual breakfast sandwich. Instead of stuffing white bread slices with bacon, egg and cheese, try this healthier alternative: toasted whole wheat bread with apple slices and melted cheese. It's sweet, savory and loaded with fiber.

Serving Size: 4

Preparation Cooking Time: 30 minutes

Ingredients:

- 1 lb. apples, cored and sliced thinly
- 2 tablespoons water
- ¼ teaspoon ground allspice
- ½ cup light cream cheese
- ½ cup cheddar cheese, shredded
- 4 whole-wheat bread slices
- ¼ cup almonds, slivered and toasted
- Cooking spray

Instructions:

1. Pour the water into a pan over medium heat.

2. Add the apples and allspice. Stir well.

3. Cover and cook for 6 minutes.

4. Uncover and cook for another 1 minute.

5. Spread the whole-wheat bread with cream cheese.

6. Top with the spiced apples, cheddar cheese and almonds.

7. Add the other whole-wheat bread slice on top.

8. Spray the sandwich with oil.

9. Toast in the oven for 3 to 5 minutes or until the cheese has melted.

10. Slice and serve.

Nutrients per Serving:

- Calories 249
- Fat 14 g
- Saturated fat 5 g
- Carbohydrates 26 g
- Fiber 8 g
- Protein 11 g
- Cholesterol 25 mg
- Sugars 13 g
- Sodium 399 mg
- Potassium 169 mg

Chocolate French Toast

If you love eating French toast for breakfast, for sure, you will also enjoy this incredible recipe that incorporates the use of chocolate, almonds and raspberries, adding more flavor and texture to your dish.

Serving Size: 2

Preparation Cooking Time: 10 minutes

Ingredients:

- 1 egg
- ½ cup almond milk (unsweetened)
- ½ teaspoon ground nutmeg
- ½ teaspoon ground cinnamon
- ¼ cup almonds, chopped and divided
- Cooking spray
- 4 slices whole-wheat bread
- 2 tablespoons chocolate syrup (sugar free)
- ¼ cup raspberries

Instructions:

1. Beat the egg in a bowl.

2. Stir in the almond milk, nutmeg and cinnamon.

3. Take ½ tablespoon almonds and set aside.

4. Add the rest to a dish.

5. Soak each of the bread slices in the egg mixture for 10 seconds.

6. Dredge both sides with the chopped almonds.

7. Toast in the oven for 6 to 8 minutes or until golden.

8. Drizzle with the chocolate syrup.

9. Sprinkle the raspberries and remaining almonds on top before serving.

Nutrients per Serving:

- Calories 250
- Fat 12 g
- Saturated fat 1 g
- Carbohydrates 29 g
- Fiber 8 g
- Protein 15 g
- Cholesterol 0 mg
- Sugars 4 g
- Sodium 391 mg
- Potassium 285 mg

Spicy Oatmeal with Egg Avocado

Obviously, this isn't your usual breakfast. This one combines your two favorites: eggs and oatmeal. You would never have imagined that your breakfast can be this exciting. You can prepare this the night before and serve it in the morning the next day.

Serving Size: 2

Preparation Cooking Time: 8 hours and 5 minutes

Ingredients:

- 1 ½ cups water
- 1 cup rolled oats
- 2 tablespoons onion
- 2 tomatoes, chopped
- ½ avocado, sliced
- 2 sunny side up fried eggs
- 2 teaspoons chili pepper sauce

Instructions:

1. Add the water into a glass jar with lid.

2. Stir in the oatmeal.

3. Seal and refrigerate for at least 8 hours.

4. Transfer the oatmeal into a bowl.

5. Arrange the onion, tomatoes, avocado and eggs on top.

6. Drizzle with the chili pepper sauce.

Nutrients per Serving:

- Calories 317
- Fat 15 g
- Saturated fat 3 g
- Carbohydrates 35 g
- Fiber 8 g
- Protein 13 g
- Cholesterol 186 mg
- Sugars 4 g
- Sodium 142 mg
- Potassium 560 mg

Sausage Breakfast Sandwich

In this sausage breakfast sandwich, we swap regular sausage with turkey sausage to make it lighter, but at the same time, maintain its great flavor. This breakfast is a healthy way to start your day.

Serving Size: 2

Preparation Cooking Time: 10 minutes

Ingredients:

- 2 multi-grain muffins
- 2 turkey sausage patties, cooked
- 2 slices cheddar cheese
- 4 teaspoons orange marmalade

Instructions:

1. Slice the muffins and toast in the oven until golden.

2. Add a slice of cheese on top of the muffin.

3. Top with the turkey sausage and orange marmalade.

4. Place the other muffin half on top.

Nutrients per Serving:

- Calories 229
- Fat 8 g
- Saturated fat 3 g
- Carbohydrates 33 g
- Fiber 8 g
- Protein 15 g
- Cholesterol 38 mg
- Sugars 7 g
- Sodium 612 mg
- Potassium 671 mg

Muesli Raspberries

Muesli is a healthier alternative to granola, which as you know is baked with oil and sugar. Top muesli with fresh raspberries to make it even more delicious.

Serving Size: 2

Preparation Cooking Time: 5 minutes

Ingredients:

- 1 cup muesli
- 1 ½ cups nonfat milk
- 2 cups raspberries

Instructions:

1. Add the muesli to a bowl.

2. Pour in the milk.

3. Top with fresh raspberries.

Nutrients per Serving:

- Calories 287
- Fat 7 g
- Saturated fat 1 g
- Carbohydrates 52 g
- Fiber 13 g
- Protein 13 g
- Cholesterol 9 mg
- Sugars 21 g
- Sodium 82 mg
- Potassium 460 mg

Oatmeal with Pine Nuts Dates

Create an incredible breakfast dish by adding dates, pine nuts, cinnamon and honey to overnight oats.

Serving Size: 2

Preparation Cooking Time: 8 hours

Ingredients:

- 1 cup water
- 1 cup rolled oats
- Salt to taste
- 2 teaspoons honey
- 2 tablespoons pine nuts, toasted
- 4 tablespoons dates, chopped
- ½ teaspoon ground cinnamon

Instructions:

1. Pour the water into a glass jar with lid.

2. Stir in the oats and season with the salt.

3. Seal and refrigerate for 8 hours.

4. Top with the rest of the ingredients before serving the next day.

Nutrients per Serving:

- Calories 281
- Fat 9 g
- Saturated fat 1 g
- Carbohydrates 48 g
- Fiber 6 g
- Protein 7 g
- Cholesterol 0 mg
- Sugars 19 g
- Sodium 150 mg
- Potassium 329 mg

Breakfast Burrito

This delicious recipe gets most of its fiber from the whole wheat tortilla while the ham, omelet, salsa and hot sauce supply it with flavor you can't get enough of.

Serving Size: 1

Preparation Cooking Time: 10 minutes

Ingredients:

- 2 tablespoons ham, cooked and chopped
- 2 tablespoons salsa
- 1 teaspoon hot sauce
- 1 egg, beaten
- 1 whole-wheat tortilla

Instructions:

1. Spray your pan with oil.

2. Add the ham and salsa.

3. Drizzle with the hot sauce.

4. Cook for 3 minutes.

5. Remove from heat and transfer to a bowl.

6. Add the egg to the pan.

7. Cook until the edges are firm.

8. Top the egg with the ham mixture.

9. Fold the egg.

10. Add the omelet on top of the tortilla.

11. Roll it up and serve.

Nutrients per Serving:

- Calories 157
- Fat 4 g
- Saturated fat 0 g
- Carbohydrates 22 g
- Fiber 13 g
- Protein 19 g
- Cholesterol 12 mg
- Sugars 4 g
- Sodium 683 mg
- Potassium 130 mg

Mixed Muesli

If you want crunchy texture in your breakfast—this is how you should do it. This recipe includes oats, wheat, barley, apple, walnuts and dried fruits. It's packed with nutrients too.

Serving Size: 4

Preparation Cooking Time: 12 hours and 30 minutes

Ingredients:

- 1 ¼ cups water
- 3 tablespoons barley (quick-cooking)
- 3 tablespoons cracked wheat
- 3 tablespoons oats
- ¼ teaspoon apple pie spice
- 1 tablespoon plain yogurt
- 1 tablespoon honey
- ½ cup nonfat milk
- Pinch salt
- 1 apple, chopped
- 1 tablespoon dried cranberries
- 1 tablespoon dried plums
- 1 tablespoon dried blueberries
- ¼ cup walnuts, toasted and chopped

Instructions:

1. Pour the water into a saucepan.

2. Stir in the barley, wheat and oats.

3. Bring to a boil.

4. Reduce heat and simmer for 8 minutes.

5. Transfer to a bowl.

6. Let cool for 5 to 7 minutes.

7. Stir in the apple pie spice, yogurt, honey, milk and salt.

8. Mix well.

9. Cover and refrigerate for 12 hours.

10. The next day, transfer mixture to a pan over low heat.

11. Cook for 3 to 5 minutes.

12. Transfer to serving bowls.

13. Top with the apples, dried fruits and walnuts.

Nutrients per Serving:

- Calories 203
- Fat 4 g
- Saturated fat 1 g
- Carbohydrates 36 g
- Fiber 7 g
- Protein 7 g
- Cholesterol 3 mg
- Sugars 16 g
- Sodium 120 mg
- Potassium 246 mg

Rosti with Bacon Tomatoes

You'll love this amazing dish—rosti with tomatoes, cheddar, bacon, oregano and zucchini.

Serving Size: 4

Preparation Cooking Time: 40 minutes

Ingredients:

- 2 eggs
- 2 slices bacon, cooked crisp and crumbled
- 1 ½ cups shredded zucchini
- Salt and pepper to taste
- 1 teaspoon oregano, chopped
- 4 cups hash browns, chopped
- 2 teaspoons vegetable oil
- 2 oz. cheddar cheese, shredded
- 1 cup tomatoes, chopped

Instructions:

1. In a bowl, beat the eggs, and stir in the bacon and zucchini.

2. Season with the salt, pepper and oregano.

3. Add the hash browns.

4. Mix well.

5. Pour oil into a pan over medium heat.

6. Add the potato mixture into the pan.

7. Cook for 10 minutes.

8. Flip and cook for another 3 minutes.

9. Sprinkle with the cheese.

10. Cook until the cheese has melted.

11. Transfer to a serving plate.

12. Sprinkle the tomatoes on top and serve.

Nutrients per Serving:

- Calories 208
- Fat 7 g
- Saturated fat 3 g
- Carbohydrates 26 g
- Fiber 4 g
- Protein 10 g
- Cholesterol 63 mg
- Sugars 2 g
- Sodium 374 mg
- Potassium 603 mg

Cinnamon Bread with Cream Cheese

As it turns out, cinnamon and cream cheese go perfectly together. You'll love this breakfast toast that you can prepare in as quickly as 5 minutes.

Serving Size: 2

Preparation Cooking Time: 5 minutes

Ingredients:

- 2 slices whole-wheat cinnamon bread
- 2 tablespoons cream cheese
- 1 teaspoon honey
- 2 slices kiwi

Instructions:

1. Toast the bread slices in the oven.

2. Spread the bread with the cream cheese.

3. Drizzle with the honey and top with the kiwi slices.

Nutrients per Serving:

- Calories 293
- Fat 8 g
- Saturated fat 4 g
- Carbohydrates 45 g
- Fiber 6 g
- Protein 8 g
- Cholesterol 20 mg
- Sugars 5 g
- Sodium 352 mg
- Potassium 350 mg

Asparagus Casserole

Even if you're not a big fan of asparagus, this dish will change your mind. Crunchy asparagus spears smothered with cheese and breadcrumbs and made more flavorful with herbs and seasonings.

Serving Size: 10

Preparation Cooking Time: 45 minutes

Ingredients:

- 3 tablespoons butter, melted and divided
- ½ cup panko breadcrumbs
- 3 lb. asparagus spears, sliced
- 1 tablespoon garlic, chopped
- 2 tablespoons all-purpose flour
- 2 cups whole milk
- ½ cup mozzarella cheese
- 5 oz. cream cheese
- Salt to taste

Instructions:

1. Preheat your oven to 450 degrees F.

2. Take 1 tablespoon butter and place in a bowl.

3. Add the breadcrumbs. Set aside.

4. Boil the asparagus in a pot of water for 1 minute.

5. Drain and rinse under cool running water.

6. Arrange these in a baking pan.

7. Add the remaining butter to a pan over medium heat.

8. Add the garlic and cook for 1 minute.

9. Stir in the flour and cook for 30 seconds.

10. Stir in the milk.

11. Bring to a boil and reduce heat to simmer for 5 minutes.

12. Stir in the mozzarella, cream cheese and salt.

13. Pour this mixture on top of the asparagus.

14. Sprinkle the breadcrumbs on top.

15. Bake in the oven for 15 minutes.

Nutrients per Serving:

- Calories 179
- Fat 11.5 g
- Saturated fat 6.6 g
- Carbohydrates 12.8 g
- Fiber 2.7 g
- Protein 7.4 g
- Cholesterol 32 mg
- Sugars 5 g
- Sodium 360 mg
- Potassium 380 mg

Fish Tostadas with Salsa

Salsa makes this seafood dish sweet and tangy. It's not that difficult to prepare too. You can make this recipe even on a busy day.

Serving Size: 4

Preparation Cooking Time: 45 minutes

Ingredients:

- 8 whole wheat tortillas
- 3 tablespoons vegetable oil, divided
- ¼ cup onion, slivered
- 6 oranges, sliced into segments
- ¼ cup cilantro, chopped
- Salt to taste
- 1 lb. cod, sliced into 4 portions
- 1 tablespoon chili and lime seasoning
- 2 avocados, mashed
- 2 cups Romaine lettuce, chopped

Instructions:

1. Preheat your oven to 400 degrees F.

2. Brush the tortillas with oil.

3. Place in the baking pan.

4. Bake for 17 minutes.

5. Let cool on a wire rack.

6. In a bowl, combine the onions, oranges and cilantro.

7. Season with the salt.

8. Rub seasoning on both sides of the fish.

9. Pour the remaining oil in a pan over medium heat.

10. Cook the fish for 3 minutes per side.

11. Spread the mashed avocado on top of the tortillas.

12. Top with the fish, orange salsa and lettuce.

Nutrients per Serving:

- Calories 572
- Fat 29.4 g
- Saturated fat 3.7 g
- Carbohydrates 54.2 g
- Fiber 14.4 g
- Protein 27.7 g
- Cholesterol 56 mg
- Sugars 20 g
- Sodium 738 mg
- Potassium 1537 mg

Grilled Broccoli with Yogurt Sauce

The secret to this recipe is to blanch the broccoli before grilling to make sure that it's tender and yet flavorful.

Serving Size: 4

Preparation Cooking Time: 25 minutes

Ingredients:

- 6 cups broccoli florets
- 4 lemon slices
- 1 teaspoon lemon zest
- Salt and pepper to taste
- 1 tablespoon olive oil
- ¾ cup Greek yogurt
- ½ teaspoon smoked paprika
- ½ teaspoon ground cumin

Instructions:

1. Fill a pot with water.

2. Bring to a boil.

3. Add the broccoli and cook for 1 minute.

4. Drain and rinse under cool running water.

5. Place a grill pan over medium heat.

6. Add the broccoli and lemon slices.

7. Grill for 3 to 5 minutes.

8. Transfer to a bowl.

9. Season with the lemon zest, salt and pepper.

10. Drizzle with the oil.

11. In another bowl, mix the yogurt and spices.

12. Serve the grilled broccoli with the yogurt sauce.

Nutrients per Serving:

- Calories 115
- Fat 6.4 g
- Saturated fat 1.7 g
- Carbohydrates 10.5 g
- Fiber 3.9 g
- Protein 7.9 g
- Cholesterol 6 mg
- Sugars 4 g
- Sodium 338 mg
- Potassium 461 mg

Corned Beef with Cabbage

Use a pressure cooker to make this dish easier to prepare. Make sure that you have everything prepared so that you'll get outstanding result. This dish is a perfect for a family feast.

Serving Size: 8

Preparation Cooking Time: 1 hour and 30 minutes

Ingredients:

- 2 tablespoons ground pickling spice
- 1 teaspoon dry mustard
- 1 ¼ teaspoons salt
- 3 lb. beef chuck roast, sliced into cubes
- 2 tablespoons vegetable oil
- 2 tablespoons vegetable oil
- 2 cups onion, chopped
- 12 oz. baby potatoes
- 1 ½ lb. carrots, sliced
- 4 cups reduced-sodium chicken stock
- 3 lb. green cabbage, sliced into wedge
- 2 tablespoons fresh dill, chopped

Instructions:

1. Mix the pickling spice with mustard and salt. Set aside.

2. In a pan over medium heat, add the beef and sprinkle with half of the pickling spice.

3. Cook for 6 to 8 minutes, stirring occasionally.

4. Transfer the beef to a bowl.

5. Add the beef, onions, potatoes and carrots in the pressure cooker.

6. Pour in the broth.

7. Stir well.

8. Top with the cabbage.

9. Seal the pressure cooker.

10. Cook on high for 30 minutes.

11. Release pressure naturally.

12. Sprinkle with the dill before serving.

Nutrients per Serving:

- Calories 385
- Fat 12.6 g
- Saturated fat 3.8 g
- Carbohydrates 30.1 g
- Fiber 8.2 g
- Protein 38.5 g
- Cholesterol 103 mg
- Sugars 12 g
- Sodium 576 mg
- Potassium 1101 mg

Italian Sausage Roasted Fennel

A feast big enough for the whole family or even when you have some friends coming over—this Italian sausage and roasted fennel recipe is not only filling but also loaded with savory flavors.

Serving Size: 12

Preparation Cooking Time: 1 hour and 35 minutes

Ingredients:

- Cooking spray
- 6 cups sourdough bread, sliced into cubes
- 2 fennel bulbs, sliced
- Salt and pepper to taste
- 2 tablespoons olive oil, divided
- 3 oz. bacon, sliced
- 1 lb. pork shoulder, sliced into cubes
- 2 teaspoons thyme, divided
- 2 teaspoons sage, divided
- ½ teaspoon ground fennel seed
- 1 ½ teaspoons whole fennel seeds
- 1 ½ teaspoons garlic, minced
- 1 cup onion, chopped
- ½ cup celery, chopped
- 1 ½ cups reduced-sodium chicken broth

Instructions:

1. Preheat your oven to 350 degrees F.

2. Spray your baking pan with oil.

3. Arrange the bread cubes in the baking pan.

4. Bake for 15 minutes.

5. Transfer the bread cubes to a bowl.

6. Increase temperature to 450 degrees F.

7. Toss the fennel in the salt, pepper and half of oil.

8. Roast in the oven for 25 minutes.

9. Transfer to a chopping board and slice.

10. Transfer to a bowl.

11. Place the bacon and pork in the food processor.

12. Pulse until chopped.

13. Add to a bowl.

14. Season with half of thyme and sage.

15. Stir in the fennel seed, garlic, salt and pepper.

16. Mix well.

17. Pour the remaining oil in a pan over medium heat.

18. Add the meat mixture.

19. Cook for 5 minutes.

20. Stir in the onion and celery.

21. Season with the remaining thyme and sage.

22. Cook for 10 minutes.

23. Pour broth into the pan.

24. Simmer for 10 minutes.

25. Transfer to a baking pan.

26. Bake in the oven for 20 minutes.

Nutrients per Serving:

- Calories 174
- Fat 7.3 g
- Saturated fat 1.8 g
- Carbohydrates 15.7 g
- Fiber 3.2 g
- Protein 10.2 g
- Cholesterol 24 mg
- Sugars 4 g
- Sodium 273 mg
- Potassium 325 mg

Teriyaki Tofu

Wild rice is not only an excellent source of fiber, it is also very easy to prepare. One pouch of cooked rice can be prepared in as quickly as 3 minutes.

Serving Size: 4

Preparation Cooking Time: 15 minutes

Ingredients:

- 20 oz. frozen wild rice in packets
- 1 tablespoon olive oil
- 18 oz. frozen stir-fry veggies
- 3 tablespoons teriyaki sauce
- 7 oz. teriyaki tofu, baked and sliced into cubes

Instructions:

1. Follow the package directions in preparing wild rice.

2. Add the wild rice to a bowl. Let cool for 5 minutes.

3. Pour the oil in a pan over medium heat.

4. Cook the vegetables for 5 minutes, stirring frequently.

5. Stir in the teriyaki sauce.

6. Coat the vegetables evenly with the sauce.

7. Remove from the stove and set aside.

8. Divide the rice in bowls or plates.

9. Top with the stir-fried veggies and tofu.

Nutrients per Serving:

- Calories 360
- Fat 8 g
- Saturated fat 1 g
- Carbohydrates 59 g
- Fiber 8.5 g
- Protein 15.2 g
- Cholesterol 102 mg
- Sugars 7 g
- Sodium 818 mg
- Potassium 30 mg

Chicken with Quinoa Veggies

This lunch or dinner bowl is packed with protein- and fiber-loaded ingredients. Not only that, it's also full of intense flavors that blend perfectly together for a satisfying meal you'd certainly love.

Serving Size: 4

Preparation Cooking Time: 30 minutes

Ingredients:

Chicken

- 5 chicken thigh fillets (skinless)
- Salt and pepper to taste

Quinoa

- 1 tablespoon olive oil
- 3 cups reduced-sodium chicken stock
- 1 ½ cups quinoa
- Salt to taste

Dressing

- 1 clove garlic
- 5 tablespoons water
- ¾ cup red-wine vinegar
- 1 tablespoon Dijon mustard
- 1 ½ tablespoons sugar
- 2 teaspoons dried oregano
- 2 teaspoons dried basil
- 1 ¾ cups olive oil
- Salt and pepper to taste

Toppings

- 15 oz. chickpeas, rinsed and drained
- 1 avocado, sliced thinly
- 5 radishes, sliced thinly
- 1 cup bean sprouts
- ¼ cup sunflower seeds

Instructions:

1. Preheat your oven to 425 degrees F.

2. Add the chicken in a baking pan.

3. Season both sides with the salt and pepper.

4. Roast the chicken for 15 minutes.

5. Slice and set aside.

6. Prepare the quinoa by adding the oil, stock and salt in a pot.

7. Bring to a boil.

8. Reduce heat and stir in the quinoa.

9. Simmer for 20 minutes.

10. Prepare the dressing by combining all dressing ingredients in a food processor.

11. Pulse until smooth.

12. Arrange the meals by dividing quinoa in serving bowls.

13. Top with the roasted chicken and the rest of the toppings.

14. Drizzle with the prepared dressing.

Nutrients per Serving:

- Calories 753
- Fat 50 g
- Saturated fat 8 g
- Carbohydrates 43.3 g
- Fiber 10.3 g
- Protein 34.3 g
- Cholesterol 76 mg
- Sugars 5 g
- Sodium 490 mg
- Potassium 836 mg

Trout with Cream Barley Sauce Herbs

Serve your trout with creamy barley sauce for an incredible lunch or dinner you and your family won't forget anytime soon.

Serving Size: 4

Preparation Cooking Time: 1 hour and 15 minutes

Ingredients:

- ½ cup parsley
- 2/3 cup leeks, chopped
- 2 cloves garlic, crushed and divided
- 1 tablespoon celery, chopped
- 1 bay leaf
- Pepper to taste
- 5 tablespoons olive oil, divided
- 1 cup pearl barley
- 4 cups water
- 4 cups reduced-sodium chicken broth
- ½ cinnamon stick
- ½ lemon
- ½ cup turnip, diced
- 2 tablespoons chives, sliced
- 2 tablespoons butter, divided
- 2 tablespoons horseradish, grated
- Salt to taste
- 4 trout fillets
- 2 sprigs fresh thyme
- 2 tablespoons tarragon
- 1 tablespoon chervil leaves

Instructions:

1. Combine the parsley, leeks, garlic, celery, pepper and bay leaf in a cheesecloth.

2. Tie with a kitchen string to secure.

3. Pound with a mallet.

4. Pour half of the oil in a pan over medium heat.

5. Cook the barley for 2 to 3 minutes.

6. Pour in the water and add the sachet.

7. Bring to a boil.

8. Reduce heat and simmer for 40 minutes.

9. Discard the herb and spice sachet.

10. Add the broth in another pan.

11. Stir in the cinnamon stick and lemon.

12. Bring to a boil.

13. Simmer for 20 minutes.

14. Strain and keep warm.

15. Pour 1 tablespoon oil in a pan.

16. Cook the turnip and carrot for 1 minute.

17. Add these to the barley along with the chives, butter and horseradish.

18. Season with the salt.

19. Transfer to a bowl and set aside.

20. Season the trout fillets with the salt and pepper.

21. Add the remaining oil in the pan over medium heat.

22. Cook the trout for 4 minutes per side.

23. Stir in the garlic and thyme.

24. Combine the remaining ingredients in a bowl.

25. Top the trout with the herbs.

26. Serve on top of the barley and broth.

Nutrients per Serving:

- Calories 646
- Fat 33.4 g
- Saturated fat 7.8 g
- Carbohydrates 48.4 g
- Fiber 9.9 g
- Protein 38.5 g
- Cholesterol 96 mg
- Sugars 4 g
- Sodium 752 mg
- Potassium 1020 mg

Cheesy Broccoli Casserole

In this quick and simple no-bake casserole recipe, you get to enjoy cheesy broccoli and rice that's loaded with flavor and awesome textures. It's ready in just 30 minutes.

Serving Size: 8

Preparation Cooking Time: 30 minutes

Ingredients:

- 1 tablespoon butter
- 8 oz. mushrooms, chopped
- 1 cup onion, chopped
- 1 tablespoon thyme, chopped
- 4 cloves garlic, crushed and minced
- 1 teaspoon Dijon mustard
- 3 ½ cups brown rice, cooked
- ½ cup sour cream
- 2 tablespoons mayonnaise
- Salt and pepper to taste
- 1 cup chicken broth (unsalted)
- 3 tablespoons cornstarch
- 3 cups broccoli florets
- 1 cup cheddar, shredded

Instructions:

1. In a pan over medium heat, add the butter, onion and mushrooms.

2. Cook for 7 to 8 minutes.

3. Stir in the thyme and garlic.

4. Cook for 1 minute.

5. Stir in the rice.

6. In a bowl, mix the sour cream, mustard, mayo, salt, pepper and broth.

7. Slowly add the cornstarch.

8. Add this mixture to the pan.

9. Add the broccoli.

10. Cover and cook for 7 minutes.

11. Sprinkle the cheese on top and cook for 1 minute.

Nutrients per Serving:

- Calories 264
- Fat 12.1 g
- Saturated fat 5.4 g
- Carbohydrates 31.7 g
- Fiber 2.7 g
- Protein 8.2 g
- Cholesterol 26 mg
- Sugars 3 g
- Sodium 301 mg
- Potassium 373 mg

Roasted Pork with Veggies Quinoa

Marinate the pork tenderloin overnight and prepare this the next day for lunch. For sure, you'll enjoy deep and intense flavors of roasted pork, balanced by the textures and savory goodness of quinoa and vegetables.

Serving Size: 4

Preparation Cooking Time: 4 hours and 45 minutes

Ingredients:

Dressing

- 1 ½ tablespoons sugar
- 5 tablespoons water
- ¾ cup red-wine vinegar
- 1 clove garlic
- 1 tablespoon Dijon mustard
- 2 teaspoons dried oregano
- 2 teaspoons dried basil
- 1 ¾ cup olive oil
- Salt and pepper to taste

Pork Veggies

- 1 lb. pork tenderloin
- 4 carrots, sliced into cubes
- 2 parsnips, sliced into cubes
- 1 broccoli, sliced into florets
- 3 tablespoons olive oil, divided
- Salt and pepper to taste
- 2 teaspoons Italian seasoning
- 4 tablespoons balsamic glaze

Quinoa

- 1 tablespoon olive oil
- Salt to taste
- 3 cups reduced-sodium chicken stock
- 1 ½ cups quinoa

Instructions:

1. Put all the dressing ingredients in a food processor.

2. Pulse until smooth.

3. Transfer to a bowl.

4. Take ¼ cup of the dressing and transfer to a sealable bag.

5. Add the pork to the bag.

6. Coat evenly with the sauce.

7. Refrigerate for 4 hours.

8. Preheat your oven to 425 degrees F.

9. In a baking pan, toss the veggies in half of the oil, salt, pepper and Italian seasoning. Set aside.

10. Roast for 20 minutes.

11. While waiting, remove the pork from the bag.

12. Season with the salt and pepper.

13. Pour the remaining oil in a pan over medium heat.

14. Cook the pork for 4 minutes per side.

15. Add to another pan.

16. Roast in the oven for 20 minutes.

17. In another pan over medium high heat, combine the oil, salt and broth.

18. Bring to a boil.

19. Stir in the quinoa.

20. Reduce heat and simmer for 20 minutes.

21. Toss the roasted vegetables with the remaining dressing.

22. Place the pork in a cutting board and slice.

23. Serve the pork with the quinoa and roasted veggies.

24. Drizzle with the balsamic glaze.

Nutrients per Serving:

- Calories 490
- Fat 21.7 g
- Saturated fat 3.5 g
- Carbohydrates 44.3 g
- Fiber 7.9 g
- Protein 15 g
- Cholesterol 74 mg
- Sugars 15 g
- Sodium 653 mg
- Potassium 1240 mg

Vegetable Wraps

Perfect for lunch, dinner or for a quick snack—this veggie wrap recipe is done in 15 minutes but loads you up with nutrients and healthy goodness.

Serving Size: 2

Preparation Cooking Time: 15 minutes

Ingredients:

- 1 avocado, sliced
- 1 teaspoon lime juice
- 1 carrot, sliced into thin strips
- 2 spinach tortillas
- 1 cucumber, sliced into thin strips
- 2 tablespoons feta cheese, crumbled
- 1 red bell pepper, sliced into thin strips

Instructions:

1. Mash the avocado in a bowl.

2. Stir in the lime juice.

3. Spread the mixture on top of the tortillas.

4. Top with the red bell pepper, carrot and cucumber strips.

5. Sprinkle the feta cheese on top.

6. Roll, slice and serve.

Nutrients per Serving:

- Calories 203
- Fat 9.6 g
- Saturated fat 1.8 g
- Carbohydrates 26.4 g
- Fiber 13.2 g
- Protein 12.5 g
- Cholesterol 6 mg
- Sugars 4 g
- Sodium 554 mg
- Potassium 460 mg

Polenta Pizza with Fresh Green Salad

Who said pizza is unhealthy? Here's a healthy way to enjoy this popular snack.

Serving Size: 2

Preparation Cooking Time: 25 minutes

Ingredients:

- 2 cups polenta, formed into rectangle
- 1 tablespoon olive oil, divided
- 4 oz. mushrooms, chopped
- 1 clove garlic, crushed and minced
- Salt to taste
- 1 teaspoon thyme, chopped
- 2 tablespoons Parmesan cheese, grated
- 2 oz. mozzarella, sliced
- ¾ cups black beans (unsalted), rinsed and drained
- 2 cups arugula
- ½ avocado, diced
- 1 tablespoon fresh parsley, chopped
- 1 ½ teaspoons lemon juice

Instructions:

1. Preheat your broiler.

2. Add 2 teaspoons oil in a pan over medium heat.

3. Cook the mushrooms for 5 minutes.

4. Stir in the garlic.

5. Season with the salt and thyme.

6. Place the polenta in the broiler. Broil for 5 minutes.

7. Sprinkle the mushrooms, Parmesan and mozzarella on top.

8. Broil for 3 minutes.

9. Toss the arugula, avocado and parsley in lemon juice and remaining olive oil.

10. Serve the pizza with the salad.

Nutrients per Serving:

- Calories 447
- Fat 22.8 g
- Saturated fat 6.1 g
- Carbohydrates 45 g
- Fiber 11.2 g
- Protein 18.2 g
- Cholesterol 24 mg
- Sugars 2 g
- Sodium 547 mg
- Potassium 838 mg

Cheese Corn on Toasted Bread

Don't have time to make yourself a snack but craving for something sweet, savory and filling? Here's one recipe that you can try—cheese, black beans and roasted corn kernels on toasted bread slices.

Serving Size: 1

Preparation Cooking Time: 10 minutes

Ingredients:

- 1 slice whole wheat bread, toasted
- 1 tablespoon black beans, rinsed and drained
- 1 tablespoon roasted corn kernels
- 1 tablespoon salsa
- 1 slice cheddar cheese

Instructions:

1. Preheat your broiler.

2. Top the toasted bread with the beans, corn and salsa.

3. Sprinkle the cheese on top.

4. Broil until the cheese has melted.

Nutrients per Serving:

- Calories 201
- Fat 6 g
- Sugars 3 g
- Saturated fat 2 g
- Carbohydrates 30 g
- Fiber 4 g
- Protein 8 g
- Cholesterol 10 mg
- Sodium 330 mg
- Potassium 351 mg

Peach Skewers

Peaches threaded through skewers with mozzarella, cherry tomatoes and basil make a great snack for the whole family.

Serving Size: 1

Preparation Cooking Time: 5 minutes

Ingredients:

- 6 cherry tomatoes
- 1 peach, sliced
- 4 basil leaves
- ¼ cup mozzarella balls

Instructions:

1. Thread the tomatoes, peaches, basil leaves and mozzarella balls into wooden skewers.

Nutrients per Serving:

- Calories 143
- Fat 5.6 g
- Saturated fat 3.1 g
- Carbohydrates 17.3 g
- Fiber 3.1 g
- Protein 7.2 g
- Cholesterol 20 mg
- Sugars 14 g
- Sodium 90 mg
- Potassium 467 mg

Lettuce Wrap Burgers

Enjoy your burger without the guilt with this healthy and delicious recipe you'd surely love to make over and over. Infusing the vegetarian burger with incredible flavors are the pickled carrots, curry paste and peanut sauce.

Serving Size: 4

Preparation Cooking Time: 30 minutes

Ingredients:

- 1 cup carrots, sliced into strips
- 3 tablespoons lime juice, divided
- 2 teaspoons chili garlic sauce, divided
- 1 cup brown rice
- 1 ½ cups edamame, shelled
- ¼ cup scallions, chopped
- ½ cup peanut butter, divided
- 2 tablespoons low-sodium soy sauce
- 1 tablespoon curry paste
- 3 tablespoons peanut oil, divided
- 4 lettuce leaves
- 1 cup onion, sliced thinly

Instructions:

1. Coat the carrots in half of chili garlic sauce and half of lime juice. Set aside.

2. Add the rice, edamame, scallions, half of peanut butter, soy sauce, curry paste and 1 tablespoon peanut oil in a food processor.

3. Pulse until chopped.

4. Form patties from this mixture.

5. Pour the remaining oil in a pan over medium heat.

6. Cook the burgers for 4 minutes per side.

7. Mix the remaining peanut butter, chili garlic and lime juice in a bowl.

8. Add the burger to the lettuce leaves, top with the carrots, onions and peanut sauce.

Nutrients per Serving:

- Calories 310
- Fat 14.5 g
- Saturated fat 1.9 g
- Carbohydrates 31.6 g
- Fiber 7.6 g
- Protein 14.6 g
- Cholesterol 102 mg
- Sugars 5 g
- Sodium 793 mg
- Potassium 473 mg

Lentil, Millet Squash

This is a healthy vegetarian recipe that you can snack on without any guilt. It's also easy to make as well. Cooking time is 8 hours but you only need 30 minutes active prep time.

Serving Size: 8

Preparation Cooking Time: 8 hours and 30 minutes

Ingredients:

- 1 cup red lentils, rinsed and drained
- ½ cup split pigeon peas, rinsed and drained
- ¼ cup millet
- 4 cups squash, sliced into cubes
- 2 teaspoons ground coriander
- 1 tablespoon chili powder
- ½ teaspoon ground turmeric
- 1 teaspoon ground cumin
- Salt and pepper to taste
- 5 cups water
- 2 tablespoons vegetable oil
- 1 teaspoon mustard seeds
- 1 teaspoon cumin seeds
- 2 cups corn kernels

Yogurt

- 2 cups plain yogurt
- ¼ cup mint, chopped
- ¾ cup cilantro, chopped
- Salt to taste

Instructions:

1. Mix the lentils, peas, millet and squash in a slow cooker.

2. Season with the coriander, chili powder, turmeric, cumin, salt and pepper.

3. Pour in the water.

4. Cover and cook on low for 8 hours.

5. Mix the yogurt, mint, cilantro and salt in a bowl.

6. Cover and refrigerate the herbed yogurt until ready to serve.

7. In a pan over medium heat, add the oil and toast the mustard seeds and cumin seeds for 30 seconds, stirring frequently.

8. Transfer the seeds to the slow cooker.

9. Add the corn kernels to the pan and cook for 3 minutes.

10. Stir into the slow cooker mixture.

11. Transfer mixture to a serving plate or bowl.

12. Top with the herbed yogurt before serving.

Nutrients per Serving:

- Calories 306
- Fat 7.7 g
- Saturated fat 3.9 g
- Carbohydrates 48.5 g
- Fiber 8 g
- Protein 14 g
- Cholesterol 15 mg
- Sugars 7 g
- Sodium 502 mg
- Potassium 826 mg

Salsa Cups

Cups made from tortilla chips stuffed with mango and papaya salsa is one snack anyone would love to devour.

Serving Size: 16

Preparation Cooking Time: 20 minutes

Ingredients:

- ¼ cup onion, chopped
- 1 ¼ cups papaya, chopped
- 15 oz. black beans, rinsed and drained
- 1 orange, chopped
- 1 cup mango, chopped
- 2 tablespoons olive oil
- 2 tablespoons freshly squeezed orange juice
- 1 tablespoon lime juice
- 2 tablespoons parsley
- Salt and pepper to taste
- 8 oz. tortilla chips shaped into cups
- Chopped cilantro

Instructions:

1. In a bowl, mix the onion, papaya, black beans, oranges and mango.

2. In another bowl, combine the olive oil, orange juice, lime juice, parsley, salt and pepper.

3. Toss the onion mixture in the olive oil mixture.

4. Serve the salsa on top of the chips.

5. Garnish with the chopped cilantro.

Nutrients per Serving:

- Calories 126
- Fat 5.3 g
- Saturated fat 0.8 g
- Carbohydrates 17.6 g
- Fiber 3 g
- Protein 2.8 g
- Cholesterol 102 mg
- Sugars 4 g
- Sodium 132 mg
- Potassium 129 mg

Caramelized Oranges

A sprinkling of sugar caramelizes oranges to create an unforgettable healthy snack that you and your family would love.

Serving Size: 4

Preparation Cooking Time: 15 minutes

Ingredients:

- 4 oranges, sliced in half (round bottoms sliced off) and seeded
- 1 teaspoon ground cardamom
- 8 teaspoons brown sugar
- 1 cup Greek yogurt

Instructions:

1. Preheat your broiler.

2. Cover your baking pan with foil.

3. Arrange the orange halves in the baking pan.

4. Mix the cardamom and brown sugar in a bowl.

5. Sprinkle the mixture on top of the oranges.

6. Broil for 5 minutes.

7. Serve the oranges with the yogurt.

Nutrients per Serving:

- Calories 168
- Fat 4.2 g
- Saturated fat 1.5 g
- Carbohydrates 26.9 g
- Fiber 2.8 g
- Protein 6.8 g
- Cholesterol 8 mg
- Sugars 24 g
- Sodium 25 mg
- Potassium 368 mg

Chicken Cauliflower Nachos

Instead of chips, this nacho recipe makes use of roasted cauliflower. It has all the flavors and crunch that you love in your nachos.

Serving Size: 4

Preparation Cooking Time: 40 minutes

Ingredients:

- Cooking spray
- 3 tablespoons avocado oil
- Salt to taste
- ¾ teaspoon chili powder
- ¾ teaspoon onion powder
- ¾ teaspoon ground cumin
- 8 cups cauliflower florets, sliced
- 1 avocado, sliced into cubes
- 2 tablespoons onion, chopped
- 1 cup tomato, chopped
- 2 tablespoons pickled jalapeño peppers, sliced
- ¼ cup cilantro, chopped
- 2 cups chicken, cooked and shredded
- ¾ cup low-sodium refried black beans
- ¾ cup Mexican cheese blend, shredded
- 1 cup cabbage, shredded

Instructions:

1. Preheat your oven to 400 degrees F.

2. Spray your baking pan with oil.

3. In a bowl, mix the avocado oil, salt, chili powder, onion powder and cumin.

4. Toss the cauliflower florets in this mixture.

5. Arrange the cauliflower in a baking pan.

6. Bake for 20 minutes.

7. Mix the avocado, onion, tomato, peppers and cilantro in a bowl.

8. Season with the salt.

9. Top the roasted cauliflower with the chicken, beans and cheese.

10. Bake in the oven for 5 minutes.

11. Serve topped with the cabbage.

Nutrients per Serving:

- Calories 487
- Fat 28 g
- Saturated fat 6.6 g
- Carbohydrates 27.2 g
- Fiber 11.2 g
- Protein 35.6 g
- Cholesterol 79 mg
- Sugars 7 g
- Sodium 484 mg
- Potassium 1238 mg

Corn Cakes

Here's another snack recipe that you'd love to make more often—corn cakes, which goes perfectly with cilantro sauce.

Serving Size: 6

Preparation Cooking Time: 35 minutes

Ingredients:

Sauce

- 1 scallion, chopped
- 1 cup cilantro, chopped
- 6 oz. Greek yogurt
- 2 teaspoons milk
- 4 teaspoons freshly squeezed lime juice

Corn cakes

- ½ cup cornmeal
- ½ cup panko breadcrumbs
- ¼ teaspoon salt
- 2 eggs, beaten
- 2 egg whites, beaten
- ¼ cup nonfat milk
- ½ cup carrot, grated
- ½ cup green bell pepper, chopped
- 2 cups corn kernels
- 2 teaspoons olive oil

Instructions:

1. Combine all the sauce ingredients in a bowl. Set aside.

2. In another bowl, mix the cornmeal, breadcrumbs and salt.

3. Stir in the eggs, egg whites, and milk.

4. Add the carrot, bell pepper and corn. Mix well.

5. Pour the oil into a pan over medium heat.

6. Pour the batter into the pan.

7. Cook for 6 minutes per side.

8. Repeat with the remaining batter.

9. Serve the corn cakes with the cilantro sauce.

Nutrients per Serving:

- Calories 187
- Fat 4.8 g
- Saturated fat 1.4 g
- Carbohydrates 27.4 g
- Fiber 2.8 g
- Protein 10.3 g
- Cholesterol 64 mg
- Sugars 6 g
- Sodium 178 mg
- Potassium 289 mg

Potato Green Beans Salad

Combine the delicious flavors of potato salad and green bean salad in one high-fiber dish that's sure to impress.

Serving Size: 6

Preparation Cooking Time: 40 minutes

Ingredients:

Dressing

- 3 tablespoons olive oil
- 1 ½ tablespoons white-wine vinegar
- ¼ teaspoon honey
- ½ teaspoon Dijon mustard
- 1 tablespoon lemon juice
- 1 teaspoon lemon zest
- 2 tablespoons dill, chopped
- Salt and pepper to taste

Salad

- 2 cloves garlic, crushed
- ½ lb. yellow potatoes, cubed
- 1 lb. red potatoes, cubed
- 1 bay leaf
- 12 oz. green beans, sliced diagonally
- Lemon slices

Instructions:

1. Combine all the dressing ingredients in a bowl. Mix well.

2. Fill a pot with water.

3. Add the garlic, potatoes and bay leaf.

4. Bring to a boil.

5. Reduce heat and simmer for 10 minutes.

6. Transfer to a bowl.

7. Discard the garlic and bay leaf.

8. Add the green beans to the pot.

9. Cook for 2 minutes.

10. Transfer the beans in a strainer and rinse.

11. Toss the potatoes and green beans in the dressing.

12. Garnish with the lemon slices.

Nutrients per Serving:

- Calories 216
- Fat 12 g
- Saturated fat 1.7 g
- Carbohydrates 25.4 g
- Fiber 3.9 g
- Protein 3.6 g
- Cholesterol 18 mg
- Sugars 4 g
- Sodium 125 mg
- Potassium 648 mg

Whole Grain Salad

In this unique salad recipe, you'll have to char the vegetables to intensify the flavors. Sumac, a popular ingredient in Middle Eastern cuisine, infuses the salad with a little bit of tartness.

Serving Size: 6

Preparation Cooking Time: 30 minutes

Ingredients:

- 5 tablespoons vegetable oil, divided
- 4 cups broccoli florets
- ½ teaspoon lemon zest
- Salt and pepper to taste
- 4 green onions
- 1 tablespoon butter
- 1 ½ teaspoons mustard
- ¼ cup parsley, chopped
- 3 tablespoons olive oil
- ½ teaspoon ground sumac
- 1 tablespoon lemon juice
- 1 tablespoon red-wine vinegar
- 2 cups cooked pearly barley
- ¼ cup radish, sliced
- ½ cup feta cheese

Instructions:

1. Put your skillet over high heat.

2. Wait until the pan is hot before you add 2 tablespoons oil.

3. Cook the broccoli until charred, turning often.

4. Transfer the broccoli to a bowl.

5. Toss the broccoli in the lemon zest, salt and pepper.

6. Reduce heat and add the green onions and butter to the pan.

7. Season with the salt.

8. Cook until charred.

9. Add these to the broccoli.

10. Put the parsley, olive oil, sumac, lemon juice and vinegar in a food processor.

11. Pulse until smooth.

12. Add the olive oil, salt and remaining vegetable oil.

13. Pulse for a few more seconds.

14. Add the barley to the broccoli mixture.

15. Stir in the radish and feta.

16. Drizzle the dressing on top.

Nutrients per Serving:

- Calories 344
- Fat 24.2 g
- Saturated fat 4.9 g
- Carbohydrates 27.1 g
- Fiber 6.3 g
- Protein 7.6 g
- Cholesterol 16 mg
- Sugars 2 g
- Sodium 484 mg
- Potassium 343 mg

Spinach Sweet Potato Salad

Pair roasted sweet potatoes, with white beans, cabbage and spinach. Toss these veggies in zesty basil dressing for a healthy salad dish you and your family can enjoy.

Serving Size: 4

Preparation Cooking Time: 40 minutes

Ingredients:

- 1 sweet potato, cubed
- Salt and pepper to taste
- 5 tablespoons olive oil, divided
- ½ cup basil
- 1 tablespoon shallot, chopped
- 3 tablespoons cider vinegar
- 2 teaspoons mustard
- 10 cups baby spinach
- 2 cups cabbage, shredded
- 1 cup red bell pepper, chopped
- 15 oz. reduced-sodium cannellini beans, rinsed and drained
- ¼ cup pecans, toasted and chopped

Instructions:

1. Preheat your oven to 425 degrees F.

2. Toss the sweet potatoes in salt, pepper and 1 tablespoon olive oil.

3. Place these in a baking pan.

4. Roast for 15 minutes.

5. Add the basil, remaining oil, salt, pepper, shallot, vinegar and mustard in a food processor.

6. Pulse until smooth.

7. Toss the sweet potatoes, spinach, cabbage, red bell pepper and beans in the dressing.

8. Sprinkle the chopped pecans on top before serving.

Nutrients per Serving:

- Calories 415
- Fat 23.6 g
- Saturated fat 2.9 g
- Carbohydrates 44.3 g
- Fiber 14.7 g
- Protein 11.8 g
- Cholesterol 75 mg
- Sugars 7 g
- Sodium 564 mg
- Potassium 498 mg

Cauliflower Salad

Roasted cauliflower drenched in lemon dressing and topped with olives, feta, parsley and almonds—an easy and delicious salad recipe you'd surely love.

Serving Size: 6

Preparation Cooking Time: 25 minutes

Ingredients:

- 8 cups cauliflower florets
- Salt and pepper to taste
- 5 tablespoons olive oil, divided
- 1 clove garlic, crushed and minced
- 1 cup parsley
- 2 tablespoons freshly squeezed lemon juice
- 3 cups arugula
- ¼ cup almonds, toasted and sliced
- ¼ cup feta, crumbled
- 2 tablespoons Kalamata olives, sliced

Instructions:

1. Preheat your oven to 425 degrees F.

2. Toss the cauliflower in the salt, pepper and 1 tablespoon oil.

3. Place the cauliflower in a baking pan.

4. Roast in the oven for 15 minutes.

5. While waiting, add the remaining oil, salt, pepper, garlic, parsley and lemon juice in a food processor.

6. Pulse until smooth.

7. Toss the cauliflower and the rest of the ingredients in the dressing.

Nutrients per Serving:

- Calories 198
- Fat 16.5 g
- Saturated fat 3 g
- Carbohydrates 10.4 g
- Fiber 4.1 g
- Protein 5.4 g
- Cholesterol 102 mg
- Sugars 4 g
- Sodium 3 mg
- Potassium 570 mg

Carrot Pea Greens Salad

In this simple recipe, you simply have to toss carrot strips and pea greens in delicious dressing you can easily make with your food processor.

Serving Size: 6

Preparation Cooking Time: 50 minutes

Ingredients:

- 1 cup chickpeas, rinsed and drained
- 1 ½ cup fresh peas, divided
- Salt and pepper to taste
- ½ cup buttermilk
- 3 tablespoons olive oil
- 25 baby carrots, sliced
- 6 carrots, julienned
- 1 cup snow peas
- 8 cups pea greens
- Lemon wedges

Instructions:

1. Mix the chickpeas, 1 cup fresh peas and salt in a food processor.

2. Pulse until smooth and set aside.

3. Mix the remaining peas with oil, buttermilk and pepper.

4. Season with the salt.

5. Add this mixture to the food processor and pulse until smooth.

6. Transfer the mixture into a bowl.

7. Toss the baby carrots, carrots, snow peas and pea greens in the dressing.

8. Serve with the reserved hummus.

9. Garnish with the lemon wedges.

Nutrients per Serving:

- Calories 214
- Fat 8.6 g
- Saturated fat 1.5 g
- Carbohydrates 27.3 g
- Fiber 8.5 g
- Protein 8.4 g
- Cholesterol 2 mg
- Sugars 12 g
- Sodium 366 mg
- Potassium 428 mg

Creamy Broccoli Soup

Aside from the broccoli, celery and leeks add unique flavor to this creamy soup. Pair it with salad, sandwich or main course.

Serving Size: 6

Preparation Cooking Time: 30 minutes

Ingredients:

- 3 tablespoons butter
- ½ cup celery, chopped
- 2 leeks, sliced
- 1 clove garlic, chopped
- 8 cups broccoli, sliced into florets
- 4 cups reduced-sodium chicken broth
- 1 teaspoon thyme, chopped
- Salt to taste
- 1 cup half-and-half
- 2 teaspoons chives, sliced thinly

Instructions:

1. Add the butter to a pan over medium heat.

2. Stir in the celery and leeks and cook for 7 minutes.

3. Add the garlic and cook for 1 minute.

4. Stir in the broccoli.

5. Pour in the broth.

6. Bring to a boil.

7. Reduce heat and simmer for 12 minutes.

8. Season with the salt and thyme.

9. Transfer the soup to a blender.

10. Puree until smooth.

11. Stir in the half-and-half and reheat for 30 seconds.

12. Top with the chives before serving.

Nutrients per Serving:

- Calories 157
- Fat 10.4 g
- Saturated fat 6.3 g
- Carbohydrates 13.4 g
- Fiber 3.5 g
- Protein 4.7 g
- Cholesterol 29 mg
- Sugars 6 g
- Sodium 351 mg
- Potassium X mg

Sweet Potato Soup

Delicious, comforting and filling—this sweet potato soup takes long hours to cook but it's definitely worth it.

Serving Size: 6

Preparation Cooking Time: 10 hours and 15 minutes

Ingredients:

- 2 cups water
- 2 cups reduced-sodium vegetable broth
- ½ cup onion, chopped
- 2 cloves garlic, crushed and minced
- 1 ½ lb. sweet potatoes, cubed
- ½ teaspoon ground cumin
- 1 teaspoon chili powder
- 1 ½ teaspoons dried oregano, crushed
- Salt to taste
- 14 oz. black beans
- 1 roasted chili pepper, sliced thinly
- 15 oz. golden hominy
- Lime wedges

Instructions:

1. Pour the water and broth into the slow cooker.

2. Add the onion, garlic, sweet potatoes, ground cumin, chili powder, oregano and salt.

3. Mix well.

4. Stir in the beans, pepper and hominy.

5. Cover the pot.

6. Cook on low setting for 10 hours.

7. Mash the sweet potatoes and put these back to the soup.

8. Garnish with the lime wedges.

Nutrients per Serving:

- Calories 202
- Fat 1 g
- Saturated fat 0.1 g
- Carbohydrates 42.1 g
- Fiber 8.5 g
- Protein 6.9 g
- Cholesterol 78 mg
- Sugars 5 g
- Sodium 491 mg
- Potassium 535 mg

Pea Buttermilk Soup

This soup gets its creaminess from tenderized peas pureed in blender. Buttermilk, meanwhile, gives it the creamy texture you'd also find worthwhile.

Serving Size: 4

Preparation Cooking Time: 30 minutes

Ingredients:

- 1 onion, chopped
- 10 oz. frozen peas
- 1 cup spinach, chopped
- 1 tablespoon fresh dill, chopped
- 14 oz. reduced-sodium chicken broth
- Salt and pepper to taste
- ½ cup buttermilk

Instructions:

1. Add all the ingredients except the buttermilk in a pot over medium high heat.

2. Bring to a boil.

3. Reduce heat and simmer for 15 minutes.

4. Let cool and then transfer to a blender.

5. Put the mixture back to the pot.

6. Add the buttermilk and simmer for 2 minutes.

Nutrients per Serving:

- Calories 83
- Fat 1 g
- Saturated fat 0 g
- Carbohydrates 14 g
- Fiber 7 g
- Protein 6 g
- Cholesterol 1 mg
- Sugars 0 g
- Sodium 423 mg
- Potassium 541 mg

Tomato Soup with Beans

Here's a unique way of preparing tomato soup: add white beans and kale. These give the classic tomato soup more flavor and texture.

Serving Size: 4

Preparation Cooking Time: 10 minutes

Ingredients:

- 28 oz. tomato soup
- 1 tablespoon olive oil
- 3 cup kale, chopped
- 1 teaspoon garlic, crushed and minced
- 14 oz. cannellini beans, rinsed and drained
- ¼ cup Parmesan cheese, grated

Instructions:

1. Prepare the tomato soup according to the directions in the package.

2. In a pan over medium heat, pour the oil and cook the kale for 1 minute.

3. Add the garlic and cook for 30 seconds.

4. Simmer for 3 minutes.

5. Sprinkle the Parmesan cheese on top before serving.

Nutrients per Serving:

- Calories 200
- Fat 5.8 g
- Saturated fat 1.4 g
- Carbohydrates 29 g
- Fiber 5.9 g
- Protein 8.6 g
- Cholesterol 4 mg
- Sugars 1 g
- Sodium 355 mg
- Potassium 257 mg

Lentil Collard Soup

Lemon, coriander and lentils come together to create this amazing soup dish that you'd love to serve to your family and friends.

Serving Size: 6

Preparation Cooking Time: 1 hour

Ingredients:

- 1 cup brown lentils, rinsed and drained
- 8 cups water, divided
- ¼ cup olive oil
- 2 onions, diced
- 2 carrots, diced
- Salt and pepper to taste
- 1 teaspoon ground coriander
- 3 cloves garlic, chopped
- ¾ cup cilantro, chopped
- 6 cups collard greens, chopped
- 1 tablespoon lemon juice
- 1 lb. potatoes, sliced into wedges

Instructions:

1. Add the lentils to a pan.

2. Pour in 3 cups water.

3. Bring to a boil.

4. Reduce heat and simmer for 30 minutes.

5. While waiting, pour the oil into a pot over medium low heat.

6. Cook the onion and carrots for 20 minutes.

7. Season with the salt and pepper.

8. Stir in the coriander and garlic.

9. Cook for 1 minute.

10. Add the cilantro and collard greens.

11. Cook for another 1 minute.

12. Pour in 1 cup water into the pan.

13. Scrape the browned bits using a wooden spoon.

14. Add the lentils and liquid, lemon juice, remaining water, potatoes and salt.

15. Bring to a boil and then simmer for 15 minutes.

Nutrients per Serving:

- Calories 296
- Fat 10.1 g
- Saturated fat 1.4 g
- Carbohydrates 42.3 g
- Fiber 7.9 g
- Protein 11.3 g
- Cholesterol 20 mg
- Sugars 4 g
- Sodium 428 mg
- Potassium 765 mg

Blueberry, Mango Kiwi Tart

Packed not only with color but also flavors and nutrients, this dessert recipe calls for topping pastry crust tofu and yogurt sauce, as well as with mangoes, blueberries and kiwi.

Serving Size: 10

Preparation Cooking Time: 2 hours and 30 minutes

Ingredients:

- 1 ¼ cups all-purpose flour
- ¼ teaspoon salt
- 3 tablespoons milk
- ¼ cup vegetable oil
- 6 oz. nonfat yogurt
- ½ teaspoon vanilla
- ½ teaspoon lemon zest
- 1 cup silken tofu
- ¼ cup lemon curd
- 1 ¼ cups mangoes, chopped
- 1 ¼ cups fresh blueberries
- 2 kiwis, chopped

Instructions:

1. Preheat your oven to 450 degrees F.

2. Mix the flour and salt.

3. Stir in the milk and oil.

4. Form a large ball from the mixture.

5. Roll out and flatten.

6. Transfer to a tart pan.

7. Trim the edges.

8. Line it with foil.

9. Bake in the oven for 8 minutes.

10. Remove foil and bake for another 5 minutes.

11. Let cool.

12. Add the yogurt, vanilla, lemon zest, tofu and lemon curd in a food processor.

13. Pulse until smooth.

14. Pour this mixture on top of the pastry.

15. Arrange the mangoes, blueberries and kiwis on top.

16. Chill in the refrigerator for 2 hours.

Nutrients per Serving:

- Calories 204
- Fat 8 g
- Saturated fat 1 g
- Carbohydrates 29 g
- Fiber 3 g
- Protein 5 g
- Cholesterol 7 mg
- Sugars 3 g
- Sodium 99 mg
- Potassium 541 mg

Apple Bars with Miso

If you think that miso is just for soup, you're wrong. You can also include it in your apple bar dessert not only to give it a unique flavor but also to balance out the taste.

Serving Size: 18

Preparation Cooking Time: 2 hours and 50 minutes

Ingredients:

- 12 tablespoons butter, divided
- 4 tablespoons white miso, divided
- 2 teaspoons vanilla
- 1 egg, beaten
- 1 cup brown sugar, divided
- ¼ teaspoon salt
- 1 teaspoon ground cardamom
- 3 cups whole-wheat flour
- 8 apples, chopped
- ½ teaspoon ground ginger
- 2 ½ tablespoons freshly squeezed lemon juice
- 1 ½ teaspoons ground cinnamon
- ½ cup pecans, chopped

Instructions:

1. Line your baking pan with parchment paper.

2. In a bowl, mix 10 tablespoons butter, half of miso, vanilla, egg and ¾ cup sugar in a bowl.

3. Beat for 2 minutes using electric mixer set on medium speed.

4. Stir in the salt, cardamom and flour.

5. Mix well.

6. Take 1 cup and refrigerate.

7. Add the rest to the baking pan.

8. Chill this for 20 minutes.

9. Preheat your oven to 350 degrees F.

10. Bake for 15 minutes.

11. Add the remaining butter and remaining miso in a pan.

12. Stir in the ¼ cup brown sugar and the rest of the ingredients except the pecans.

13. Cook for 15 minutes.

14. Add these on top of the crust.

15. Sprinkle the pecans on top.

16. Bake in the oven for 30 minutes.

17. Slice and serve.

Nutrients per Serving:

- Calories 244
- Fat 10.2 g
- Saturated fat 5.1 g
- Carbohydrates 36.3 g
- Fiber 3.8 g
- Protein 3.6 g
- Cholesterol 31 mg
- Sugars 18 g
- Sodium 161 mg
- Potassium 127 mg

Fruit Cups

Give a treat to your sweet tooth without the guilt with this frozen fruit cup recipe that's ready in a few minutes.

Serving Size: 8

Preparation Cooking Time: 4 hours and 45 minutes

Ingredients:

- 2 cups cantaloupe, chopped
- 2 cups strawberries, chopped
- 1 cup fresh raspberries
- 1 cup fresh blackberries, sliced in half
- 2 tablespoons sugar
- ½ teaspoon lemon zest

Instructions:

1. Mix all the ingredients in a food processor.

2. Pulse until smooth.

3. Transfer the mixture to a container.

4. Freeze for 4 hours.

Nutrients per Serving:

- Calories 53
- Fat 0.4 g
- Saturated fat 0 g
- Carbohydrates 12.8 g
- Fiber 3 g
- Protein 1 g
- Cholesterol 18 mg
- Sugars 10 g
- Sodium 7 mg
- Potassium 322 mg

Strawberry Brownies

Up the ante of your favorite fudge brownies by adding chopped strawberries on top.

Serving Size: 12

Preparation Cooking Time: 1 hour

Ingredients:

- Cooking spray
- 12 oz. chocolate brownie mix
- ¼ cup pecans, chopped
- ½ cup applesauce
- 1 cup strawberries, chopped
- 3 tablespoons vegetable oil
- 1 egg, beaten
- 1 oz. chocolate

Instructions:

1. Preheat your oven to 350 degrees F.

2. Spray your baking pan with oil.

3. In a bowl, mix the brownie mix, pecans, applesauce, half of strawberries, vegetable oil and egg.

4. Beat the mixture using a wooden spoon.

5. Pour the batter into a baking pan.

6. Sprinkle remaining strawberries on top.

7. Bake for 35 minutes.

8. Melt chocolate in a pan over low heat.

9. Drizzle on top of the brownies.

Nutrients per Serving:

- Calories 165
- Fat 9 g
- Saturated fat 0.9 g
- Carbohydrates 27.1 g
- Fiber 3.7 g
- Protein 2 g
- Cholesterol 1 mg
- Sugars 2 g
- Sodium 98 mg
- Potassium 49 mg

Choco Banana Ice Cream Pops

Banana ice cream covered with chocolate and peanut butter is certainly a great way to cap your meal or to freshen up during a hot summer day.

Serving Size: 8

Preparation Cooking Time: 6 hours and 30 minutes

Ingredients:

- ¼ cup water
- ¼ cup peanut butter
- 3 bananas, sliced
- Pinch salt
- 9 oz. chocolate chips, melted

Instructions:

1. Add the water, peanut butter, bananas and salt in a food processor.

2. Pulse until smooth.

3. Pour the mixture into popsicle molds.

4. Freeze for 6 hours.

5. Remove the popsicles from the molds.

6. Dip in the chocolate.

7. Freeze for 5 minutes.

Nutrients per Serving:

- Calories 272
- Fat 15 g
- Saturated fat 6.6 g
- Carbohydrates 35.2 g
- Fiber 4 g
- Protein 4.3 g
- Cholesterol 34 mg
- Sugars 25 g
- Sodium 57 mg
- Potassium 318 mg

Green Smoothie

Make this healthy smoothie by blending bananas, avocados and kale, and stirring in chia seeds. It's not only packed with fiber, but also with omega 3 fatty acids.

Serving Size: 1

Preparation Cooking Time: 5 minutes

Ingredients:

- ¼ ripe avocado
- 1 cup kale, chopped
- 1 banana
- 1 cup vanilla-flavored almond milk
- 2 teaspoons honey
- 1 tablespoon chia seeds
- 1 cup ice cubes

Instructions:

1. Add the avocado, kale, banana, almond milk, honey and chia seeds in a blender.

2. Blend until smooth.

3. Add the ice cubes.

4. Pulse until ice cubes are crushed.

Nutrients per Serving:

- Calories 343
- Fat 14.2 g
- Saturated fat 1.6 g
- Carbohydrates 54.7 g
- Fiber 12.1 g
- Protein 5.9 g
- Cholesterol 0 mg
- Sugars 29 g
- Sodium 199 mg
- Potassium 1051 mg

Minty Berry Kefir Smoothie

Like yogurt, kefir is known for its beneficial probiotics, which are good for maintaining digestive health. In this recipe, you'll add kefir to your mint and berry smoothie.

Serving Size: 2

Preparation Cooking Time: 35 minutes

Ingredients:

- ¼ cup strawberries
- ¼ cup blueberries
- ¼ cup raspberries
- 1 cup reduced-fat plain kefir
- 1 tablespoon honey
- 1 tablespoon fresh mint leaves
- ¼ cup freshly squeezed orange juice

Instructions:

1. Add the strawberries, blueberries, raspberries, kefir, honey, mint leaves and orange juice in a blender.

2. Pulse until smooth.

3. Chill in the refrigerator for 30 minutes before serving.

Nutrients per Serving:

- Calories 137
- Fat 1 g
- Saturated fat 1 g
- Carbohydrates 27 g
- Fiber 7 g
- Protein 6 g
- Cholesterol 5 mg
- Sugars 15 g
- Sodium 64 mg
- Potassium 997 mg

Ginger Mango Smoothie

Ginger adds a little zing to your favorite mango smoothie in this quick and simple recipe that's ready in 5 minutes.

Serving Size: 1

Preparation Cooking Time: 10 minutes

Ingredients:

- 1 cup mango, sliced into cubes
- 1 teaspoon ginger, chopped
- ¾ cup carrot juice
- ½ cup red lentils, cooked
- 1/8 teaspoon ground cardamom
- 1 teaspoon honey
- ¼ cup ice cubes

Instructions:

1. Place the mango, ginger, carrot juice, red lentils, ground cardamom, honey and ice cubes in a blender.

2. Blend until smooth.

Nutrients per Serving:

- Calories 352
- Fat 1.1 g
- Saturated fat 0.2 g
- Carbohydrates 78.9 g
- Fiber 9.6 g
- Protein 12.3 g
- Cholesterol 10 mg
- Sugars 41 g
- Sodium 122 mg
- Potassium 787 mg

Cranberry Blueberry Smoothie

This power smoothie is loaded with so many nutrients that you can be sure that it's one of the healthiest ways to start your day.

Serving Size: 1

Preparation Cooking Time: 5 minutes

Ingredients:

- 1 banana
- 1 cup cranberries
- 1 cup blueberries
- 1 cup nonfat plain kefir

Instructions:

1. Mix all the ingredients in a blender.

2. Pulse until smooth.

3. Refrigerate for at least 1 hour before serving.

Nutrients per Serving:

- Calories 245
- Fat 1.3 g
- Saturated fat 0.2 g
- Carbohydrates 50.4 g
- Fiber 8 g
- Protein 12.5 g
- Cholesterol 5 mg
- Sugars 34 g
- Sodium 3 mg
- Potassium 337 mg

Carrot Cake Smoothie

If you love carrot cake, you can be sure that you're going to enjoy this refreshing and nutritious smoothie.

Serving Size: 1

Preparation Cooking Time: 10 minutes

Ingredients:

- ¾ cup coconut milk
- 1 cup carrot, chopped
- ½ cup pineapple chunks
- ½ cup apple, chopped
- 1 teaspoon vanilla
- 1 date, pitted
- ¼ teaspoon pumpkin pie spice
- ¼ cup rolled oats
- 3 ice cubes
- 1 tablespoon coconut flakes

Instructions:

1. Combine all the ingredients except the coconut flakes in a blender.

2. Process until smooth.

3. Refrigerate for 30 minutes.

4. Sprinkle with the coconut flakes before serving.

Nutrients per Serving:

- Calories 315
- Fat 5.5 g
- Saturated fat 3.3 g
- Carbohydrates 65.5 g
- Fiber 10.7 g
- Protein 4.8 g
- Cholesterol 12 mg
- Sugars 38 g
- Sodium 92 mg
- Potassium 845 mg

Conclusion

Now that you're done reading the book, you can see that there are countless high-fiber recipes that you can prepare at home without any difficulty.

Always keep in mind that fiber is an essential part of a healthy diet. By including these high-fiber dishes in your weekly menu, you can maintain a healthy digestive system. At the same time, you can help keep serious ailments such as heart disease and diabetes at bay.

Author's Afterthoughts

I want to convey my big thanks to all of my readers who have taken the time to read my book. Readers like you make my work so rewarding and I cherish each and every one of you.

Grateful cannot describe how I feel when I know that someone has chosen my work over all of the choices available online. I hope you enjoyed the book as much as I enjoyed writing it.

Feedback from my readers is how I grow and learn as a chef and an author. Please take the time to let me know your thoughts by leaving a review on Amazon so I and your fellow readers can learn from your experience.

My deepest thanks,

Sophia Freeman

https://sophia.subscribemenow.com/

Printed in Great Britain
by Amazon

27771913R00101